THE STOCK MARKET CRASH OF 1929

GREAT DEPRESSION FOR KIDS

HISTORY BOOK 5TH GRADE

Children's History

I n this book, we're going to talk about the Stock Market Crash of 1929. So, let's get right to it!

During the 1920s, the United States had a decade of prosperity. World War I had ended and there was an economic boom brought about by a huge increase in manufacturing as well as new technologies. The radio, the automobile, and the airplane were changing

Crowd of excited traders at stock exchange.

the way people lived. The stock market began to soar and people felt as if nothing could go wrong. Unemployment was only 3% and most people were making enough money to have a good lifestyle.

A night out.

THE ROARING TWENTIES

Throughout the 1920s, the stock market began to increase by leaps and bounds. The Dow Jones Industrial Average, which is an index of the average of top stocks used to give a measure of the economy, increased from 60 to 400. In other words, the economy had increased over six times what it had been at the beginning of the 1920s. This economic boom and the wild cultural boom it created was nicknamed *"The Roaring Twenties."*

The huge increase in the economy had made many people millionaires. Money was flowing and investors bought more and more stocks. At that time, no warning bells were being sounded because most financial analysts felt that the economy was solid since industry was doing so well. Investors thought their money was safe and that the stock market would continue to rise. Stock trading had become like a *"get rich quick"* pastime. People were mortgaging their homes and investing all their savings into stocks like Ford Motor Company and RCA Victor.

Nightclub in the 1920's

H owever, most average investors really didn't understand their own investments. They hadn't studied the finances or underlying business processes and didn't truly comprehend the risk factors. Criminals formed fake companies designed to trick unsuspecting investors and it worked. People bought these investments in a mad grab to make as much money as possible.

Crowd in a bank.

Adding more risk to the situation was that investors were also buying stocks on margin. This means that they were borrowing money from their stockbrokers to buy stocks. It's a form of loan that allows the investor the ability to buy even more stock than he or she could normally purchase.

90
80
70
60
90
80
70
60
50
ENGLISH
SO
SC

For example, for every $100 invested, an investor buying on margin could borrow $900 worth of stock. If a stock increased 1% in value, instead of just making a 1% profit, the investor would make 10% because of this additional leverage.

Stock market panic.

It was a way for investors to quickly multiply the profit on their investments, without investing all their own cash. However, what most investors didn't realize is that buying on margin works the opposite way as well. If their stock lost value instead of gained, they could lose all the money they invested and could owe money back to the broker too!

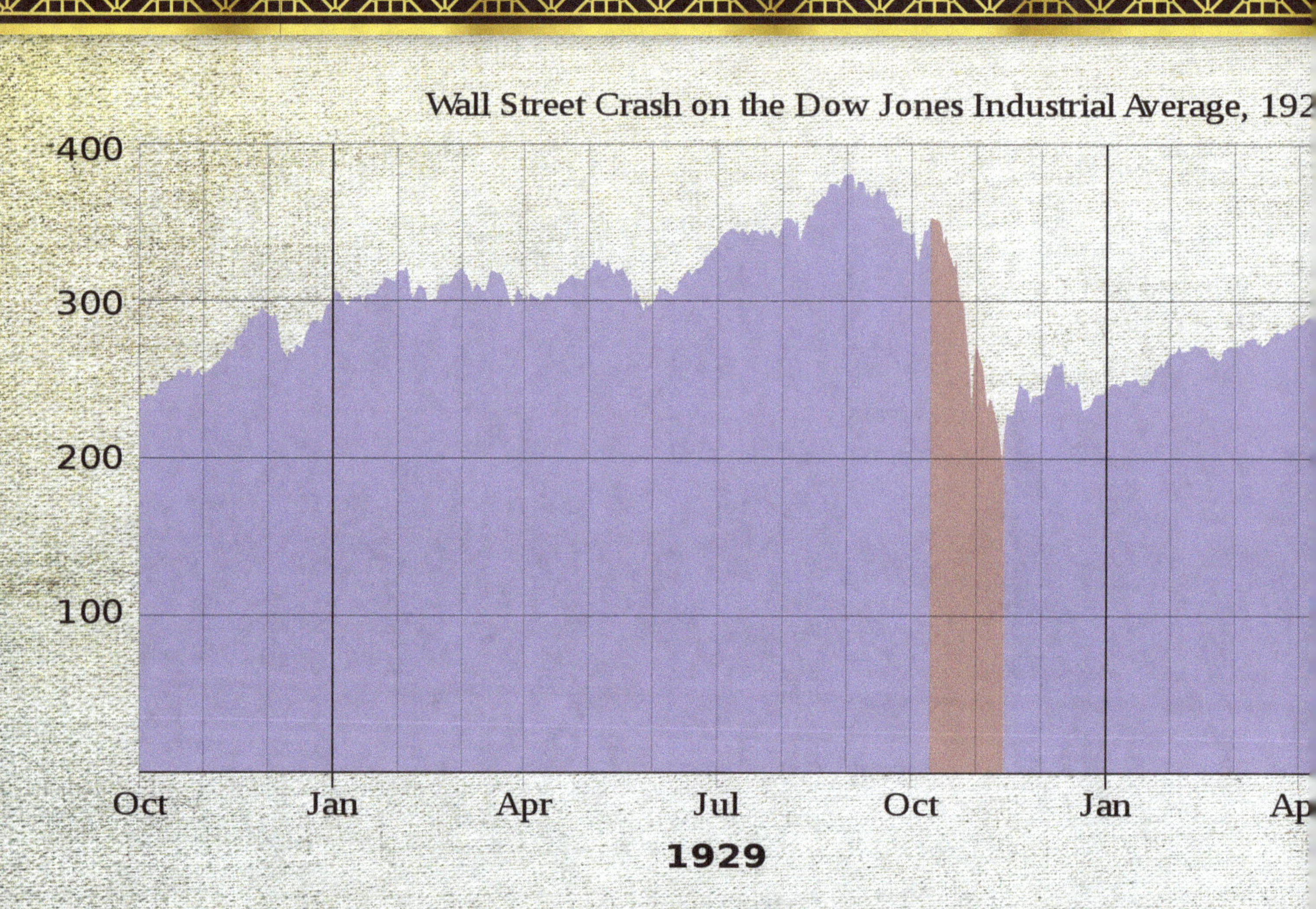

A stock market bubble was happening. Over a period of time, when investors

1930

1929 Wall Street crash graph.

drive prices of stocks much higher than they should be valued, then it's called a stock market bubble. Bubbles eventually burst. That's what happened when the *"Roaring Twenties"* came to an abrupt end on Thursday, October 24th in 1929. On that day, the stock market came crashing down.

HOW DID THE STOCK MARKET CRASH HAPPEN?

When events and investments in the stock market cause stock prices to rise, it's called a bull market. When stocks decrease in value over time and people become worried about the economy, then a bear market has set in. Concerned about the very fast pace of increase in the stock market, the Federal Reserve increased the rate of interest several times in 1929.

TWELVE
SEVEN
EIGHT
TEN
NINE
TWELVE
THIRTEEN

This was in an effort to cool the over-heated market, but by October the stock market had gone into decline and a bear market had started.

Then, on that fateful Thursday, a huge panic occurred and people starting to sell their stocks all at once. Over 12 million stock shares were traded on that day, which was eventually called Black Thursday.

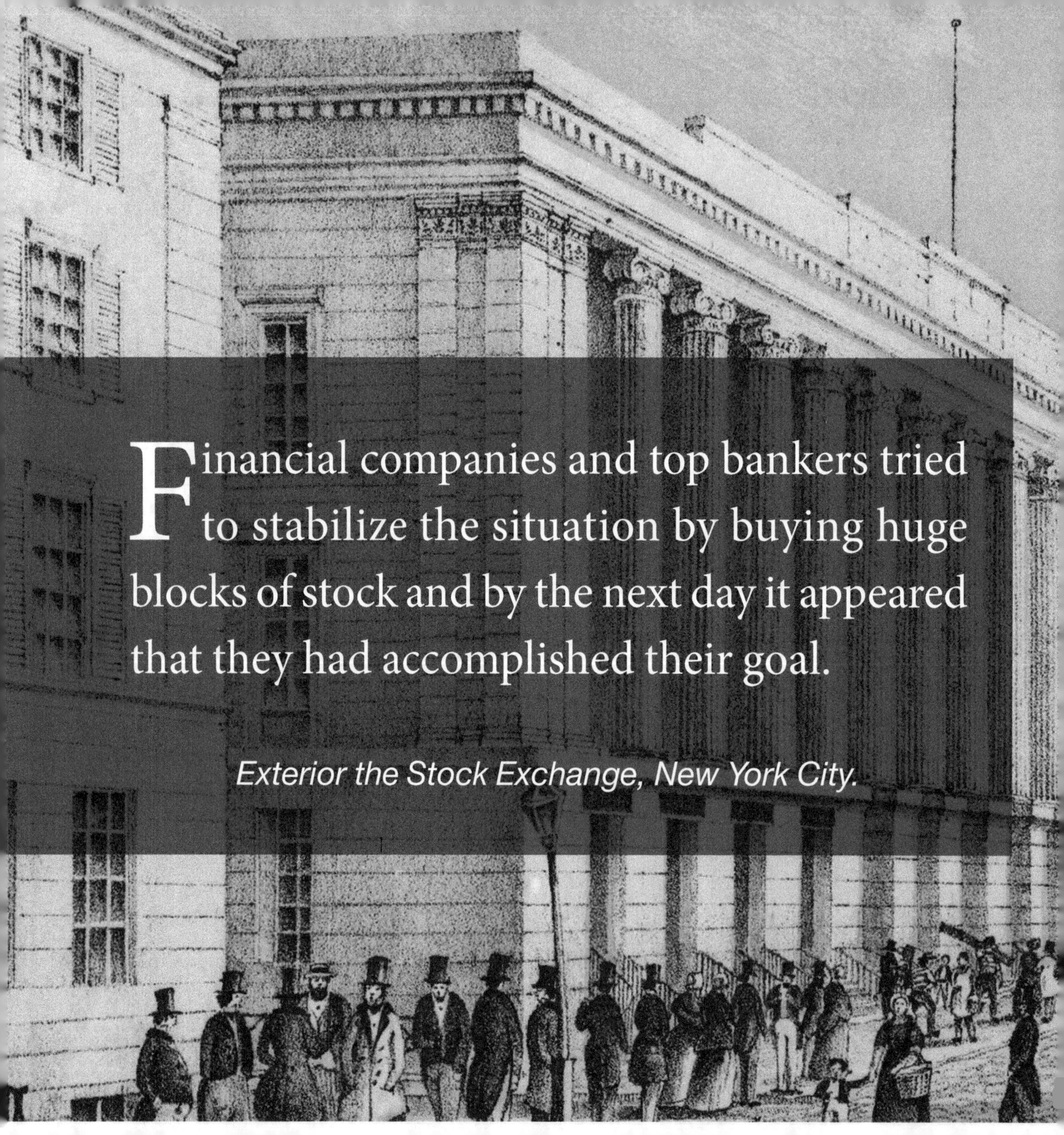

Financial companies and top bankers tried to stabilize the situation by buying huge blocks of stock and by the next day it appeared that they had accomplished their goal.

Exterior the Stock Exchange, New York City.

Crowds in the lobby of new bank in Detroit.

However, by Monday, intense fear had set in as people realized what was happening. The values of the stocks they had purchased were over-inflated and weren't really worth what people had thought they were worth. Everyone was selling and no one was buying. Black Monday, October 28th and Black Tuesday, October 29th brought the complete collapse of the stock market. That Tuesday over 16 million shares were traded. It would be another 40 years before this many shares were traded in one day again.

Millionaires went bankrupt overnight. Billions of dollars had been lost and thousands of investors were ruined.

The market continued to sink through November of that year. By the end of the crash, over $16 billion dollars had been lost from the stocks on the New York Stock Exchange.

Stock traders on the floor of the New York Stock Exchange in 1936.

To make the situation even worse, many banks had been using bank deposits to make investments in the stock market. There were runs on the banks as patrons all showed up at the same time to take their savings out. Many banks and financial institutions went bankrupt. The entire financial structure of the United States was in chaos.

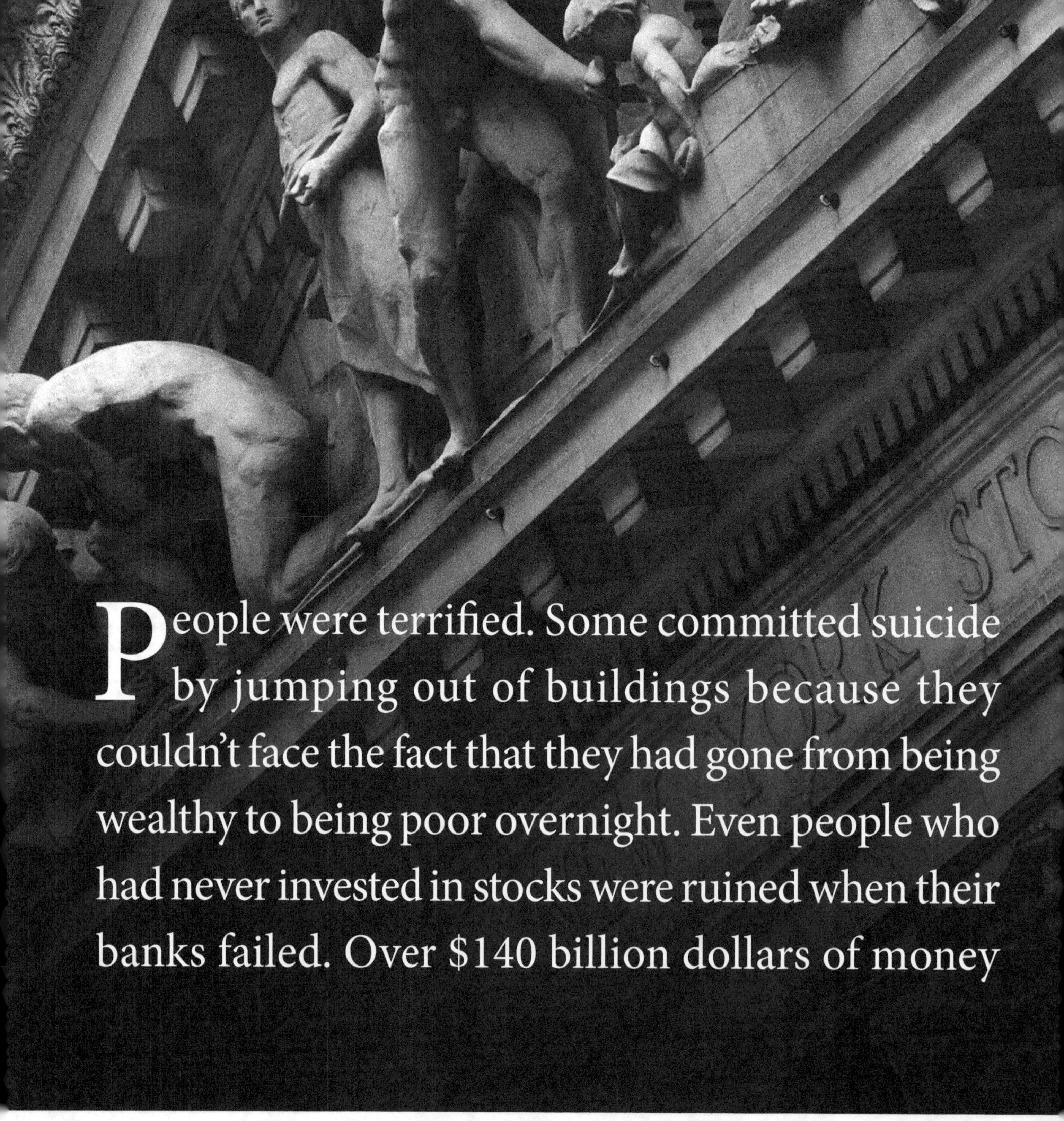

People were terrified. Some committed suicide by jumping out of buildings because they couldn't face the fact that they had gone from being wealthy to being poor overnight. Even people who had never invested in stocks were ruined when their banks failed. Over $140 billion dollars of money

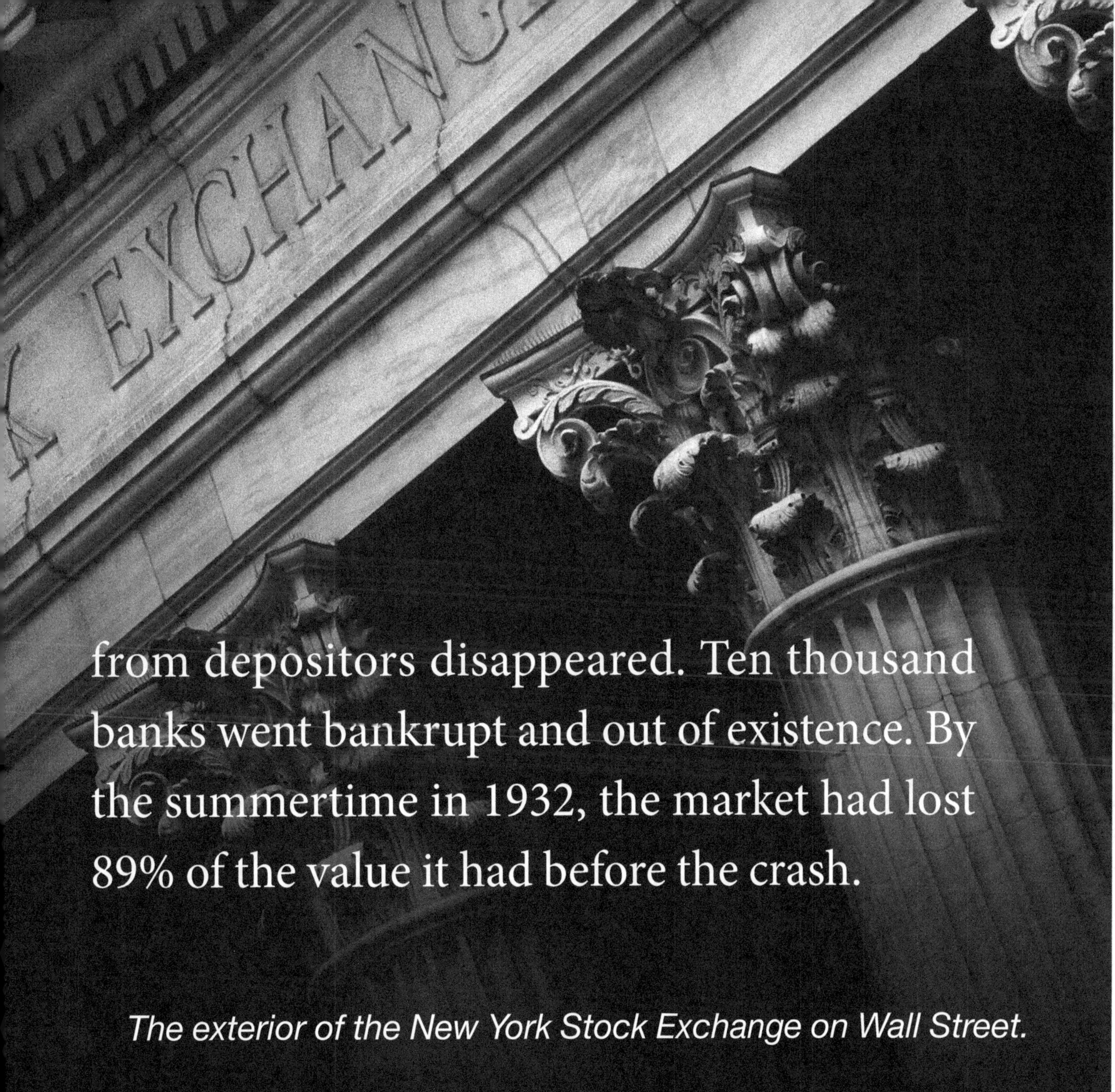

from depositors disappeared. Ten thousand banks went bankrupt and out of existence. By the summertime in 1932, the market had lost 89% of the value it had before the crash.

The exterior of the New York Stock Exchange on Wall Street.

DID EVERYONE LOSE MONEY?

S ome investors made the right decisions just in time. Jesse Lauriston Livermore, a self-made millionaire correctly predicted the crash and made over 100 million dollars due to his quick action. He made and lost several fortunes throughout his life.

Joseph Kennedy, father of John F. Kennedy and Robert Kennedy, also sold his stocks in time to retain his wealth. He had heard some shoeshine boys and other novice investors talking about investing in the market. It dawned on him that this would only be true during a bubble, so he quickly sold his stocks before the crash.

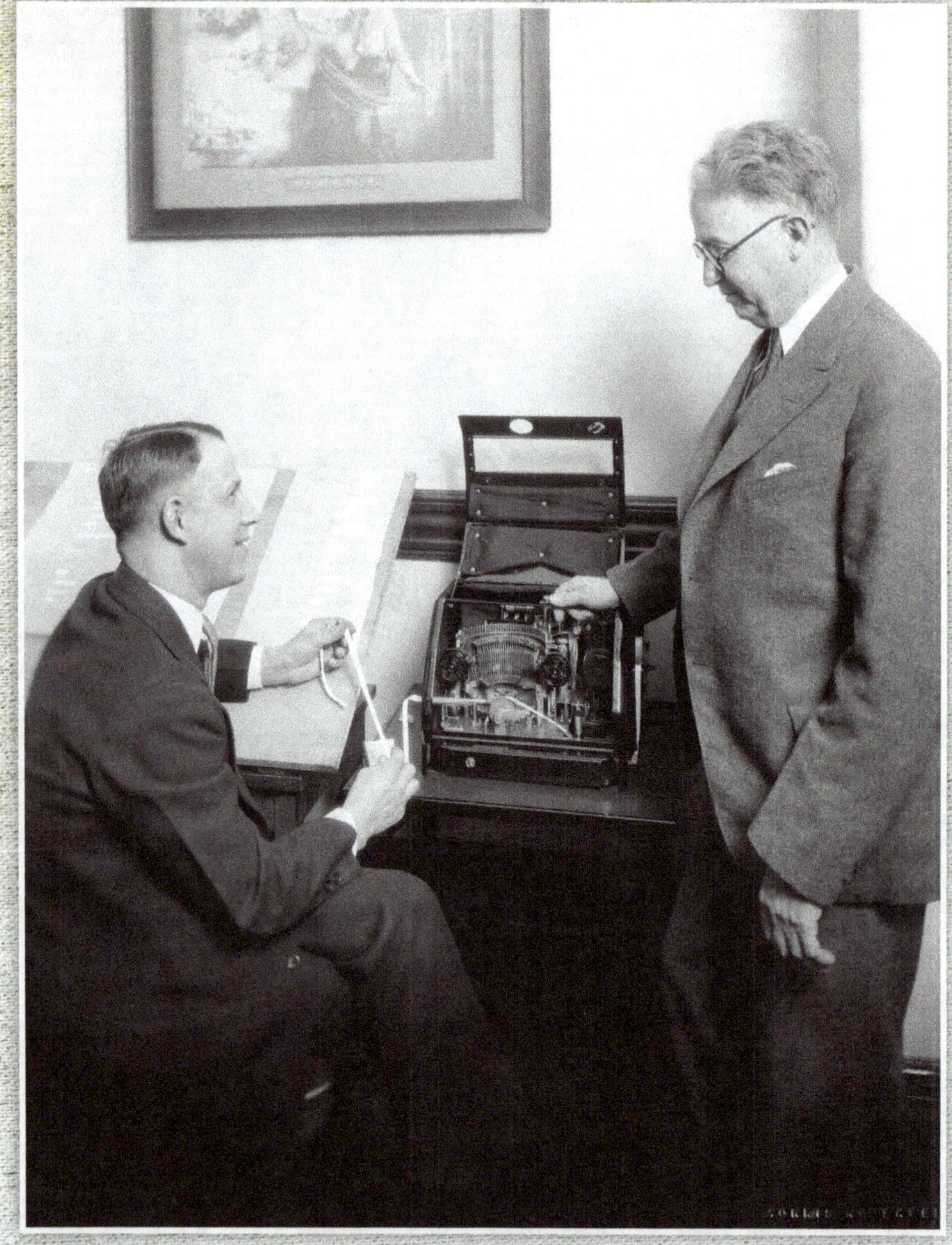

Stock brokers with a new box shaped stock ticker in May 1929.

WHAT CAUSED THE GREAT DEPRESSION?

There were many reasons for the Great Depression. Historians as well as economists cite these as the top five reasons:

THE STOCK MARKET CRASH OF 1929

The Stock Market Crash had a powerful impact on the American people. Even though the stock market started to come back, it wasn't enough economic recovery and by the end of 1930, the Great Depression had begun in earnest.

BANK FAILURES

Thousands of banks failed and savings accounts evaporated. The banks that survived stopped lending money to people. This made it nearly impossible to start a business or keep a failing business open long enough to recover.

Stock brokers using a stock ticker, 1929.

Financier J.P. Morgan Jr., after testifying before the Senate Banking and Currency Committee. May 23, 1933.

PEOPLE STOPPED BUYING THINGS

Because people had lost so much money or because they had lost their jobs or both, they couldn't buy anything new. Factories and businesses couldn't sustain themselves because no one was buying their goods and services. This led to a vicious cycle because businesses couldn't afford to keep the workers they had. Many people had bought items on installment plans before the crash. They couldn't make their payments so their items were repossessed.

ECONOMIC POLICY WITH EUROPE

To protect American companies, the Smoot-Hawley Tariff was passed in 1930. This placed high taxes on imports from Europe, which made people reluctant to purchase these goods. Less trade between America and other countries caused other problems, some of which led to World War II.

Traders bidding on commodity futures, Sept. 1939.

DROUGHT CONDITIONS

The drought in the Great Plains was not a direct cause, but it was economically devastating for the farmers in the Dust Bowl. They couldn't grow corps so they couldn't pay their debts or taxes. Many abandoned their farms or sold them for no profit.

Soil blown by dust bowl winds piled up in large drifts on a Kansas farm. March 1936. Photo by Arthur Rothstein

Hunger Marchers breakfast just outside Washington DC, December, 1932.

BOSSES GOVERNMENT
FIRST AVENUE VAN CO
OFFICE 97 E.3rd ST. N.Y.C.
RELIABLE
REASONABLE

THE GREAT DEPRESSION

The crash of the stock market was the start of the Great Depression. People went from riches to rags. This difficult time in United States history lasted for over 10 years. One fourth of the entire population was out of work and over 30% of the population was living in poverty. Thousands of businesses went bankrupt and couldn't recover.

Unemployed men wait in line to file Social Security benefit claims. In January 1938.

CALIFORNIA HOSPITAL.

Many people became homeless and had to live in shantytowns. They blamed President Herbert Hoover for the depression and called the towns *"Hoovervilles"* after him.

In urban areas, people stood in very long lines to get a cup of soup to eat. In the countryside, farmers were struggling to get their crops to grow. A huge drought had caused the topsoil to turn to dust and enormous dust storms traveled across the Great Plains.

EQUAL JUSTICE
W.P.A. TECHNICIANS CAN PLAN & BUILD Low Cost HOMES
WPA

WPA protest march in front of the U.S. Supreme Court, Jan. 16, 1937.

WHEN DID THE STOCK MARKET RECOVER?

Once it reached rock bottom in 1932, the market began to make a very slow recovery. The Great Depression ended when the Second World War began in 1939. The economy improved during the war because factories needed workers. However, it wasn't until 1955 before the stock market came back to the peak value it had had before the crash.

The Great Depression. Itinerant worker, traveling by foot.

ING
ROAD

N ow you know more about the Stock Market Crash of 1929 and the resulting Great Depression. You can find more History books from Baby Professor by searching the website of your favorite book retailer.

Visit
BABY PROFESSOR
EDUCATION KIDS
www.BabyProfessorBooks.com
to download Free Baby Professor eBooks
and view our catalog of new and exciting
Children's Books